ARTIFICIAL INTELLIGENCE
COLLECTION

FUNDAMENTALS

THE ESSENTIALS FOR MASTERING ARTIFICIAL INTELLIGENCE

Prof. Marcão – Marcus Vinícius Pinto

Disclaimer:

Please note that the information contained in this document is for educational and entertainment purposes only. Every effort has been made to provide complete, accurate, up-to-date, and reliable information. No warranty of any kind is express or implied.

By reading this text, the reader agrees that under no circumstances are the authors liable for any losses, direct or indirect, incurred as a result of the use of the information contained in this book, including, but not limited to, errors, omissions, or inaccuracies.

ISBN: 9798341178649

Publishing imprint: Independently published

Summary

Welcome!

In recent years, Artificial Intelligence (AI) has established itself as one of the most exciting and innovative areas of computer science and technology.

The ability of machines and algorithms to learn, reason, and make decisions autonomously is profoundly transforming various industries and driving exponential advances in several areas.

The book "Artificial Intelligence – Fundamentals" fills a fundamental gap by presenting the reader with a comprehensive and accessible view of the main concepts, applications and challenges faced in the era of Artificial Intelligence.

An integral part of Prof. Marcão's Artificial Intelligence Collection, this volume complements an exclusive group of books focused on data governance and AI, all available on Amazon digital platforms.

From the importance of information as an essential raw material to the discussion of ethics, data privacy, and the promising future of this technology, each chapter addresses in a clear and detailed way fundamental aspects to understand AI and its impact on society.

By following the historical evolution of AI, from its beginnings to today's representatives and advanced large-scale language models, the reader will be taken on a fascinating journey through the historical milestones and technological innovations that have shaped the current AI landscape.

The topics covered in this book, such as Machine Learning, Natural Language Processing, Computer Vision, Ethics and Transparency in AI Projects, among others, have been carefully selected to provide a comprehensive and up-to-date view on AI.

In addition, the discussion about the importance of data, the correct structuring of databases, and the ethical and legal challenges faced in the implementation of AI projects provide valuable insights for professionals and researchers in the field.

Through clear explanations, practical examples, and a didactic approach, this book aims to guide the reader through the vast and dynamic field of Artificial Intelligence, providing essential knowledge and comprehensive perspectives for those who wish to understand, apply, and explore the full potential and possibilities offered by this revolutionary technology.

Additionally, sections dedicated to data security and privacy, ethics, and legal compliance reflect the growing importance of addressing these issues responsibly and transparently in the development and implementation of AI systems.

The work also highlights the relevance of data quality and reliability, emphasizing the need to properly structure databases to ensure accurate and reliable results in AI projects.

With detailed case studies, such as chat GPT, the reader will have the opportunity to explore in practice how data structuring and modeling can directly impact the performance and safety of AI systems.

As Artificial Intelligence continues to play an increasingly central role in our daily lives, understanding the challenges, ethical implications, and opportunities associated with this technology becomes essential for everyone involved in its development, implementation, and regulation.

This book not only offers a deep dive into the essential concepts and practical applications of Artificial Intelligence, but also fuels reflections on the future of this discipline and its impact on society and humanity as a whole.

I invite you, dear reader, to venture into the pages of this book and explore a universe of knowledge and discoveries in the fascinating world of Artificial Intelligence.

May this work be an inspiring and informative source to guide you through the complexities and promises of AI, contributing to a greater understanding and mastery of this powerful and transformative technology.

I wish you good reading, good learning and good projects.

Prof. Marcão - Marcus Vinícius Pinto

M. Sc. in Information Technology
Specialist in Information Technology.
Consultant, Mentor and Speaker on Artificial Intelligence,
Information Architecture and Data Governance.
Founder, CEO, teacher and
pedagogical advisor at MVP Consult.

1 Between synthetic minds and emerging realities.

Artificial intelligence (AI) transcends the mere creation of machines capable of performing human cognitive tasks. It delves into deep philosophical questions that go back to antiquity, where thinkers like Aristotle were already wondering about the nature of the mind and rationality.

AI, as we know it today, is the result of centuries of philosophical, mathematical, and scientific progress, culminating in a field of study that seeks not only to replicate, but in many cases to surpass human capabilities.

1.1 The philosophical bases: from discards to the digital age.

The French philosopher René Descartes, with his famous cogito, ergo sum ("I think, therefore I am"), laid the groundwork for mind-body duality, a dichotomy that influences debates about the creation of synthetic minds to this day.

AI, in many ways, challenges this dichotomy, proposing the possibility of intelligence in non-biological entities.

Another important philosophical milestone was the work of Alan Turing, whose proposition of the "Turing Test" suggested that intelligence could be assessed on the basis of observed behavior, regardless of the nature of the entity exhibiting it (TURING, 1950).

This concept opened doors to the design of machines that could be considered intelligent if their actions were indistinguishable from those of a human being.

1.2   Evolution and classical approaches in AI.

The first steps of AI were marked by symbolic systems, also known as symbolic AI, where the focus was on manipulating symbols and explicit rules to solve problems.

Herbert Simon and Allen Newell, pioneers in this approach, developed programs such as the Logic Theorist and the General Problem Solver, which attempted to mimic human reasoning processes (SIMON, 1957).

However, these systems proved limited, mainly because they relied on manually coded rules and were unable to handle the ambiguity and uncertainty present in the real world.

With the advancement of computational capabilities, AI has evolved to incorporate statistical and probabilistic techniques, giving rise to machine learning.

This transition was crucial, as it allowed machines to learn from data, rather than relying on pre-programmed rules.

Supervised learning, where models are trained on labeled data, and unsupervised learning, where the structure of data is discovered without explicit labels, have become central pillars of modern AI.

Geoffrey Hinton, Yoshua Bengio, and Yann LeCun are some of the researchers who have revolutionized the field with their contributions to deep neural networks, a sub-area of machine learning that emulates the architecture of the human brain (HINTON et al., 2015).

1.3   Artificial neural networks: the brain of machines.

Artificial neural networks (ANNs) are inspired by the structure and functioning of the human brain. Composed of layers of artificial neurons, these networks have the ability to learn complex patterns from large amounts of data.

ANNs are the foundation of deep learning, a technique that has revolutionized areas such as image recognition, machine translation, and natural language processing.

One of the milestones in the evolution of ANNs was the development of convolutional networks (CNNs) by LeCun et al. (1989), which proved to be extremely effective in computer vision tasks.

In addition to CNNs, recurrent neural networks (RNNs) have brought significant advances in the processing of sequential data, such as text and time series.

However, traditional RNNs faced challenges such as the disappearance of the gradient, which limited their ability to learn long-term dependencies. This problem was mitigated with the introduction of Long Short-Term Memory (LSTM) by Hochreiter and Schmidhuber (1997), allowing networks to better capture these dependencies.

1.4   Natural language processing: the intersection between language and AI.

Natural language processing (NLP) seeks to empower machines to understand, interpret, and generate human language in a meaningful way.

From the early days of NLP, with approaches based on formal grammar, to modern deep learning techniques such as Transformers and pre-trained models such as GPT (Generative Pretrained Transformer), there has been a significant evolution.

The work of Vaswani et al. (2017) in the development of Transformer was a game-changer, eliminating the need to resort to recurrent networks to capture long-range dependencies in text sequences.

GPT, developed by Radford et al. (2018), exemplifies the potential of NLP. This model is capable of generating coherent text, translating languages, and even answering questions in a contextualized way.

However, the use of these models also raises important ethical issues, such as the potential to perpetuate biases present in training data (BENDER et al., 2021).

1.5   6. AI in Practice: Real Examples and Applications

AI is already transforming a variety of industries, from healthcare to finance. In healthcare, for example, AI algorithms are used to diagnose diseases from medical images with accuracy comparable to or superior to that of human physicians (LITJENS et al., 2017). In the financial sector, AI is being applied to detect fraud, optimize investment portfolios, and predict market trends.

In education, AI-based adaptive systems personalize learning for each student, adjusting content and difficulty based on individual performance.

These systems not only improve learning outcomes but also support educators, allowing for a more effective and student-centered approach (KUMAR et al., 2020).

In the field of security, AI is being used to monitor large volumes of data in real time, detecting patterns that could indicate suspicious activity or imminent cyberattacks. These applications demonstrate how AI can increase efficiency and safety in complex, high-demand environments.

1.6   7. The Ethical Challenge: AI and Human Responsibility

The increasing integration of AI into various spheres of human life raises ethical questions that cannot be ignored. Issues of privacy, security, transparency, and accountability are at the heart of debates about the future of AI. The ability of machines to make decisions that affect human lives requires careful examination of the moral implications of such technologies.

The biases present in training data, which can lead to discrimination in AI systems, are a clear example of how technologies can perpetuate and amplify existing inequalities (NOBLE, 2018).

In addition, the increasing autonomy of machines calls into question responsibility for the actions taken by AI systems, especially in critical contexts such as criminal justice and public safety.

2   Fundamentals of artificial intelligence.

Artificial Intelligence (AI), at its core, refers to systems or machines that mimic human intelligence to perform tasks and progressively improve based on the information they gather.

This multidisciplinary field crosses areas such as computer science, psychology, philosophy, neuroscience, among others, to create machines capable of reasoning, perception and learning.

2.1   AI applications.

The applications of AI are diverse and cut across all sectors of society, including:

1. Health. Faster and more accurate diagnoses, predictions of disease outbreaks, personalization of treatments, and automation of administrative tasks.
2. Transport. Autonomous vehicles, route optimization and traffic management.
3. Finance. Fraud detection systems, risk management, robo-advisors for investment advice and operations automation.
4. Retail. Personalization of the customer experience, optimization of inventory, and prediction of market trends.
5. Manufacturing. Predictive equipment maintenance, supply chain management, and production line automation.

2.2   Data Requirements for AI.

For AI systems to work and learn, they need data, often in large quantities. This data is used to train machine learning algorithms, which are the heart of most AI applications.

The three fundamental pillars on data requirements for AI include.

1. Data Volume. AI, especially deep learning, requires large volumes of data to identify patterns and make accurate predictions. This is often referred to as 'big data'.

2. Data Quality. The quality of the data influences the accuracy of the AI's results. This encompasses the accuracy, completeness, relevance, and timeliness of the data.

3. Variety of Data. AI needs a variety of data to capture the complexity of the real world and offer very generalized results. This includes structured data (such as database tables), unstructured data (such as free text, images, audio, and video), and semi-structured data (such as emails or formatted documents).

4. Labeled data. For supervised learning methods, it's crucial to have labeled data, that is, data where observations are linked to known labels or responses that the algorithm can use to learn and make predictions.

5. Data Diversity. The data should cover a diverse range of cases and scenarios in order to reduce bias and ensure that AI can function properly under diverse conditions.

6. Shareable Data. Privacy and legality issues must be considered to ensure that data can be shared with AI systems ethically and in accordance with current regulations, such as GDPR.

7. Data recorded temporarily. For problems such as time series analysis or when the chronology is significant, the data needs to be correctly annotated with timestamps.

Data quality and variety are key to avoiding the problem of 'garbage in, garbage out' (GIGO), where low-quality input data in AI training leads to low-quality results.

It is essential that the data used in the training not only fairly represents all affected groups but is also free from bias that could lead to discrimination or injustice.

In addition to data, AI systems also require advanced algorithms, powerful computer architecture (such as specialized GPUs for processing neural networks), and software frameworks and mathematical libraries that enable the deployment and training of AI models.

2.3   AI Development and Training

Developing an AI system requires clear problem definition, data collection and cleaning, choosing a suitable machine learning model, training the model with a dataset, and evaluating its effectiveness.

Once trained, the AI model is tested with a new dataset (the test set) to verify its ability to generalize and make predictions or make decisions based on previously unseen data.

There are several methods and techniques used in the AI training process, including:

1. Supervised Learning. Where models are trained on a dataset with known labels. They learn to predict output from the inputs provided.

2. Unsupervised Learning. Where models look for patterns in labelless data, such as customer segmentation in marketing.

3. Reinforcement Learning. A model learns through trial and error, maximizing a reward or minimizing a punishment during training.

4. Neural Networks and Deep Learning. Complex structures that mimic the way the human brain processes information, effective especially in tasks such as speech and image recognition.

2.4 Challenges of AI.

Despite significant progress in AI, several challenges remain, including:

5. Bias and Justice. AI systems can perpetuate or even amplify biases present in training data.

6. Explainability and Transparency. Many AI models, especially deep neural networks, are considered 'black boxes' and offer little understanding of how decisions are made.

7. Data Privacy. AI models can reveal sensitive or personal information contained in the training data.

8. Safety. AI systems can be vulnerable to attacks, such as examples of adversity designed to fool AI models.

2.5   Future of AI.

As we move forward, the field of AI will continue to evolve, with significant implications for innovation, society, and ethics.

Continuous research and development in Artificial Intelligence aims to overcome current challenges and expand its capabilities. Approaches to increasing the explainability and transparency of models, such as explainable AI (XAI), are becoming increasingly important as AI is adopted in high-risk areas such as healthcare and case law, where it is vital to understand the rationale behind decisions made by AI.

Furthermore, techniques for mitigating bias and promoting fairness in AI are a rapidly expanding field, with multidisciplinary teams working to develop fairer and more representative algorithms.

To ensure data privacy, developers are exploring techniques such as federated learning, where AI models are trained without sensitive data having to leave the user's device, and homomorphic encryption, which allows data to be processed while encrypted.

AI security is also a focus of intense research, involving building anomaly detection systems to identify and respond to malicious input, and developing robust AI architectures that can withstand attacks without compromising performance.

As AI continues to advance, the debate around AI legislation and regulation also advances. This seeks to ensure that your application is safe, transparent, and fair.

Organizations and governments around the world are recognizing the need for regulatory frameworks that not only encourage innovation in AI but also protect the rights of individuals and promote the well-being of society at large.

AI is increasingly being applied in areas such as climate change, where it can help model complex climate predictions, analyze large environmental datasets, and optimize systems to reduce energy consumption.

It is also seen as a critical enabler for sustainable development, helping to find solutions to the UN Sustainable Development Goals in areas such as agriculture, health, energy, and natural resource conservation.

Because AI can process and analyze large volumes of environmental data and make faster, more accurate predictions, it can accelerate research into renewable energy, improve water use efficiency in agriculture with the use of sensors and AI, and provide deeper analysis of biodiversity patterns for conservation efforts.

The concept of 'AI for good' focuses on the development and application of AI technologies to address major humanitarian issues and solve global problems. This includes projects ranging from AI assistants that help people with disabilities to advanced AI systems that track and respond to natural disasters.

While AI continues to develop, consideration of fundamental issues such as ethics, privacy, security, and fairness remains crucial.

Industry, academia, governments, and international organizations must collaborate to create a future where AI is employed to improve people's lives and sustain global development, while ensuring that we remain vigilant against the risks and challenges that may arise.

This requires a holistic, interdisciplinary approach that considers not only the science and technology behind AI, but also the complexities of the human and social context in which it operates.

3   Basic concepts and definitions.

Artificial Intelligence (AI) is emerging as one of the most significant technologies of the twenty-first century. From handling massive data to mimicking human cognitive processes, AI has expanded its roots in many fields.

Artificial intelligence (AI) has become one of the fundamental pillars of technological metamorphosis in the contemporary market. It builds on the concept that machines, especially computer systems, can be taught to simulate aspects of human intelligence—a view that translates into the definition presented by Russell and Norvig (2016), who consider it as "the study of the agent who receives perceptions of the environment and performs actions". However, the current context of rapid technological evolution and market demands has broadened and refined this vision.

Today's AI is more than just an agent perceiving and acting; It is deeply rooted in systems that inform and shape decision-making in sectors ranging from healthcare and finance to e-commerce and urban management.

Human abilities to learn, reason, and self-improve are only the beginning. Modern machines, with the aid of AI, are now able to predict trends, personalize experiences, and interact with users on a virtually limitless scale.

In today's market, AI has become an essential element to sustain and increase competitive differential. With the explosion of data available, organizations turn to AI systems that can process and analyze this data efficiently, offering insights that drive business strategies, optimize operational processes, and improve the customer experience.

To stay ahead, professionals need to consider the following important tips when integrating artificial intelligence into their operations:

1. Understand your business needs.

   Evaluate how AI can address specific problems and add value. Don't adopt AI for your sake; Focus on solutions that respond to concrete challenges.

2. Prioritize data quality.

   AI systems are only as good as the data they receive. Ensure that your data is clean, relevant, and well represents the problems to be solved. Inaccurate or biased data can lead to erroneous conclusions and hinder AI-based decision-making.

3. Incorporate ethics from the start.

   AI brings ethical challenges, especially regarding privacy and bias. It is crucial to implement ethical practices in the development and application of AI involving considerations about the social impact of deployed technologies.

4. Educate your team.

   Investing in training and education is vital. Employees at all levels must understand the capabilities and limitations of AI so that they can work effectively with this technology.

5. Consider AI as a complement, not a substitute.

AI should be seen as a tool that enhances human capabilities, not replaces them. The goal is to increase efficiency and effectiveness, freeing up humans to focus on creative and strategic tasks.

6. Explore AI-as-a-service solutions.

   For businesses that don't have the skills or resources to develop their own solutions, AI-as-a-service can be an effective and less risky option by leveraging third-party expertise.

7. Adaptability and flexibility.

   The market and technologies are constantly changing. AI systems that adapt and learn from new data and conditions are essential to maintaining relevance in the market.

8. Ensure safety.

   AI solutions must be secure against breaches, ensuring data integrity and users' trust in systems.

9. Integration with other technologies.

   AI does not operate in a vacuum. Its integration with other emerging technologies like big data, IoT, and blockchain can unlock new levels of efficiency and innovation.

10. Track the impact of AI.

    Monitor the performance and results of AI systems after implementation, adjusting strategies and processes as needed to ensure that they remain aligned with business objectives and stakeholder expectations.

11. Long-Term Planning.

Implementing AI requires thinking ahead, considering not only the immediate impact, but also how it will evolve and scale within your organization in the future.

12. User-Centered Design.

When developing AI applications, focus on the user experience. Technology must be intuitive and add value without creating barriers or unnecessary complexity.

13. Cross-Industry Collaboration.

Collaboration across different industries and disciplines can lead to more robust innovations and more effective AI solutions. Interdisciplinarity brings new perspectives and unexpected solutions.

14. Examine legal issues.

Understand and comply with local and international laws and regulations related to AI, such as privacy and data protection regulations.

15. Promote transparency.

The decisions made by AI systems must be explainable, both to build trust in users and to facilitate continuous improvement of the system.

AI is transforming the business landscape in ways that were unimaginable just a few decades ago. The ability to not only emulate, but also extend and enhance human abilities, defines the new generation of AI solutions.

Companies that strategically implement AI and follow best practices are positioned to take advantage of the opportunities that this revolutionary technology offers.

By doing so, they can enjoy improved operational efficiencies, better data insights, and a competitive advantage in the globalized marketplace.

3.1   Main categories.

The basic concepts of AI can be understood through four main categories, as follows.

3.1.1   MACHINE LEARNING.

Machine learning is indeed one of the most fascinating pillars of artificial intelligence, and the definition offered by Alpaydin (2020) encapsulates the essence of this revolutionary technology.

This branch of AI is responsible for systems that can not only perform programmed tasks, but also continuously improve their performance through experience – just like humans.

In more technical terms, machine learning employs statistical algorithms to build mathematical models based on raw data. These models are designed to identify patterns and make inferences or predictions.

To better understand this process, let's imagine a machine learning program as a young apprentice, who instead of reading books or listening to classes, studies large data sets to gain knowledge.

Just as a student can learn to identify features of a particular artistic style by studying many paintings, a machine learning algorithm can learn to recognize patterns and features in digital data.

These systems become increasingly skilled at identifying patterns and making predictions as they are fed more data.

For example, product recommenders on e-commerce platforms get better at suggesting relevant items the more information they have about a user's shopping preferences.

Machine learning is at the forefront of numerous contemporary technological innovations, including predictive analytics in finance, computer-aided medical diagnostics, autonomous vehicle systems, and more.

In addition, with the advent of deep learning, a subfield of machine learning, machines can now recognize and interpret images and audio, even understanding natural language, which enhances the application in an even wider range of contexts.

The core idea is that rather than relying on rigid rules and detailed programming for each specific task, these systems rely on pattern recognition and inferential logic

3.1.2   Natural language processing (NLP).

Machine learning is indeed one of the most fascinating pillars of artificial intelligence, and the definition offered by Alpaydin (2020) encapsulates the essence of this revolutionary technology.

This branch of AI is responsible for systems that can not only perform programmed tasks, but also continuously improve their performance through experience – just like humans.

In more technical terms, machine learning employs statistical algorithms to build mathematical models based on raw data. These models are designed to identify patterns and make inferences or predictions.

To better understand this process, let's imagine a machine learning program as a young apprentice, who instead of reading books or listening to classes, studies large data sets to gain knowledge.

Just as a student can learn to identify features of a particular artistic style by studying many paintings, a machine learning algorithm can learn to recognize patterns and features in digital data.

These systems become increasingly skilled at identifying patterns and making predictions as they are fed more data.

For example, product recommenders on e-commerce platforms get better at suggesting relevant items the more information they have about a user's shopping preferences.

Machine learning is at the forefront of numerous contemporary technological innovations, including predictive analytics in finance, computer-aided medical diagnostics, autonomous vehicle systems, and more.

In addition, with the advent of deep learning, a subfield of machine learning, machines can now recognize and interpret images and audio, even understanding natural language, which enhances the application in an even wider range of contexts.

The core idea is that rather than relying on rigid rules and detailed programming for each specific task, these systems rely on pattern recognition and inferential logic to solve problems.

This allows them to adapt to new and unseen situations during training, which is a hallmark of so-called generalized intelligence, as opposed to the more limited and specific forms of artificial intelligence.

The power of machine learning also lies in its ability to demystify large data sets – known as big data – by finding correlations and causalities where traditional analysis might not reveal or would be extremely time-consuming and costly to be performed by humans.

Not only does this significantly broaden the applicability of AI across multiple domains, but it also highlights the ability of machine learning to unlock new insights and knowledge.

However, machine learning is not without its challenges. Issues such as bias in data – where algorithms can replicate or exacerbate existing disparities – are the subject of intense debate and ongoing research to ensure fairness and fairness in automated systems.

In addition, the more complex the machine learning model becomes, the more difficult it can be for humans to understand exactly how decisions are made, a phenomenon known as the "black box."

In response to these challenges, a field of study has emerged focused on making AI algorithms more interpretable and explainable.

The idea is to build systems that can not only make accurate predictions, but that can also convey to their human users how those predictions were made. This is crucial for the acceptance and responsible use of AI in critical contexts such as medical care, justice systems, and public safety.

Machine learning, therefore, continues to be a dynamic field within artificial intelligence, with transformative potential for numerous industries.

As technology advances, its ability to process information and simulate aspects of human intelligence is also expected to continue to grow, leading to an ever-increasing and more innovative adoption of AI in our daily lives and work.

3.1.3   Computer vision and robotics.

Computer vision is a field of study within artificial intelligence that empowers computers to interpret and understand the visual world in the same way that humans do.

Forsyth's (2020) description highlights the complexity and sophistication of this function: it allows AI-equipped systems to translate images and visual sequences into understandings that can guide independent actions.

By simulating human visual perception, computer vision is employed in a variety of practical applications. Autonomous vehicles are an example where cameras and sensors capture visual information that is then interpreted by AI systems for navigation and decision-making on the road.

These systems must not only "see" their environment, but also understand the relevance of other vehicles, pedestrians, traffic signs, and the varied road conditions.

In surveillance systems, computer vision is used to detect unusual activities, identify individuals or objects, and even for behavior analysis.

This technology also supports more natural and intuitive interactions between humans and machines, such as the interpretation of gestures and facial expressions, making interaction with devices and user interfaces more fluid and responsive.

In addition, computer vision also has significant applications in other domains, such as:

1. Health. To aid in medical diagnosis by analyzing X-ray images, MRIs, and other medical images.

2. Agriculture. Monitoring crops via drones to check plant health and need for water or nutrients.

3. Trade. Recognizing products and enabling checkout systems without the need for queues.

4. Industry. Automated inspection for quality control and automation of processes that require detailed visual evaluation.

The quality and accuracy of computer vision depend to a large extent on the training data and algorithms applied. The more visually diverse data the system is able to process and learn, the more accurate it tends to be in its operations.

Convolutional neural networks (CNNs), a type of deep learning neural network that specializes in recognizing visual patterns, are often utilized for complex computer vision analysis.

These networks simulate the way human vision identifies features in a hierarchical sequence of increasing complexity: from lines and edges to shapes and finally to entire objects.

To maximize the potential of computer vision, researchers and developers work not only to improve the accuracy and efficiency of these systems, but also to make them more understandable and reliable.

This involves continuously improving data training techniques, developing robust algorithms against harsh conditions (such as variable lighting or visual obstructions), and implementing measures to ensure ethics and fairness in the recognition and processing of facial and behavioral features.

An additional aspect is the importance of explainability in computer vision models.

The ability of systems to not only perform tasks, but also to explain their decisions and processes in terms understandable by humans, is a field of research known as XAI (Explainable Artificial Intelligence).

This is particularly relevant in critical areas where automated decisions can have significant impacts on people's lives, such as safety and medicine.

With the rapid evolution of technology, computer vision continues to open new frontiers for innovation and application of AI making the partnership between machines and humans not only more productive, but also more natural and effective.

3.1.4   Robotics.

The combination of Artificial Intelligence (AI) with mechanical and electrical engineering, as highlighted by Murphy (2019), is indeed a significant advance in the field of robotics.

Robots with advanced cognitive capabilities can make real-time decisions based on their perception of their environment. They are capable of performing autonomous movements and tasks, which means they can operate without direct human guidance.

This breakthrough is a game-changer in industrial manufacturing, where intelligent robots can enhance manufacturing capabilities.

These machines not only work with greater precision and efficiency, but also reduce safety risks, as they can take over dangerous or repetitive tasks that were previously performed by human workers.

What's more, intelligent robotics is a powerful tool in the hands of explorers and scientists. With it, humanity can go beyond physical limitations and explore previously inaccessible environments. Notable examples include probes and vehicles sent into space, which are capable of collecting data on other planets without human presence.

In the underwater context, intelligent robotics allows the study of deep ocean ecosystems, biodiversity monitoring, and mineral resource assessment without exposing humans to the inherent risks of these environments.

The rise of autonomous systems is also present in contexts such as agriculture, with autonomous robotic tractors and harvesters that can plant, monitor, and harvest with little or no human assistance.

In disaster response contexts, intelligent robots can be used for search and rescue, navigating through rubble or reaching areas that would be too dangerous for human rescue teams.

Smart robotics is therefore not only a fascinating field with far-reaching practical applications, but also a showcase of the possibilities that arise from merging the computational power of AI with the physical and functional design of robotic systems.

By adding advanced perception, data processing, and autonomous decision-making capabilities, robots are now more adaptable and able to handle varying uncertainties and complexities.

In addition to expanding exploratory horizons and increasing safety, intelligent robots are also revolutionizing customer service, with personal assistants and home assistance devices improving daily life in countless ways.

They can, for example, clean spaces, offer useful information, and even care for more vulnerable members in our families.

In healthcare, AI-equipped robots are transforming surgical procedures, enabling minimally invasive operations with superhuman precision.

In educational settings, robots can provide personalized support to students, adapting to their pace and learning style.

Despite these advances, there are substantial challenges related to the development and deployment of intelligent robotics.

Issues such as integrating systems into human environments in a safe and ethical manner, creating regulations that govern their use, and the need to educate professionals to work side-by-side with these new technologies require serious consideration.

Additionally, it is crucial to address the implications on the labor market, as automation can significantly alter the demands for skills and the nature of employment.

As we move forward, multidisciplinary collaboration between engineers, computer scientists, ethicists, policymakers, and other professionals will be essential to fully harness the benefits of intelligent robotics while maintaining a commitment to sustainable and inclusive development.

The interplay between AI and robotics promises not only new developments in the way we perform tasks, but also a reimagining of our own potential as creators and users of technology.

3.2   Decision algorithms.

Decision algorithms represent a fundamental aspect of artificial intelligence, allowing computerized systems to make choices without the need for direct human intervention.

The insights of Shalev-Shwartz and Ben-David (2014) underscore the crucial role of these methods in a variety of critical scenarios.

Essentially, a decision algorithm uses data inputs to produce an output or decision by applying machine learning rules and statistics to evaluate the available options.

Although the processes and complexity behind these decisions can vary enormously, in general, algorithms aim to maximize efficiency, accuracy, and effectiveness, whether when diagnosing a disease, choosing which actions to invest in, or even defining the best allocation of resources in a public policy.

In the field of healthcare, decision algorithms are transforming the diagnosis and treatment of medical conditions. AI-powered systems analyze medical test data and patient histories to identify patterns that may indicate certain diseases.

In the financial sector, these algorithms are used to analyze markets, predict stock trends, and manage investment portfolios with a speed and volume of data far beyond human capability.

When it comes to public policy, AI can help policymakers understand the potential consequences of their plans by modeling and predicting the outcomes of different scenarios.

For example, decision algorithms can be used to optimize the distribution of limited resources, such as the allocation of funds for education or for natural disaster response, ensuring that they are used as effectively as possible.

However, as decision algorithms gain prevalence, important concerns also arise. Incorrect or biased data can lead to flawed decisions, perpetuating injustices or causing material and human damage. Therefore, the transparency, explainability, and accountability of algorithms are essential aspects to be addressed.

Transparency refers to how algorithms work and how they are built. It is essential that users and those affected by the decisions of these systems are clear about the mechanisms and factors involved in decision-making.

In addition, the explainability of algorithms is crucial; It is not enough for a machine to be able to make decisions, it is necessary for these decisions to be understandable by humans, especially when they have significant consequences. This becomes even more important in regulated industries such as healthcare and finance, where automated decisions need to go through audits and compliance.

Accountability is another key factor, as with the growth of decision automation comes the question of who is responsible when something goes wrong.

Are the developers of algorithms, the entities that use them, or the algorithms themselves? Because AI systems are developed by humans, the ultimate responsibility often lies with the creators or operators of technology.

The conscious development of decision-making algorithms implies ensuring that AI is used ethically, fairly and without bias. This often requires a multidisciplinary effort, bringing to the table ethicists, jurists, sociologists, and other professionals, in addition to traditional engineers and computer scientists.

Finally, decision algorithms are not just technical tools; They embody values, norms, and goals of their creators and the social context in which they are implemented. Therefore, when developing and deploying such algorithms, it is vital to consider not only the technical and operational aspects, but also the social and moral impact they will have.

Artificial intelligence, therefore, is not just a matter of computational efficiency; It is also a matter of human choices and social influence, reflecting the challenges and responsibilities in our ongoing pursuit of progress and well-being through technology.

3.3   Ethical issues.

However, AI also raises ethical issues, especially in relation to data privacy and work automation. Harari (2018) argues that

"AI could lead to an unprecedented disruption in human history, possibly redefining work and the global economy."

This points to the importance of regulations and an informed public debate about the responsible and ethical development of AI.

Harari's quote touches on crucial aspects of the spread of AI, which lies at the junction between the promise of extraordinary breakthroughs and profound ethical and societal challenges.

Concerns about data privacy and the impact of automation on work are just a few of the ethical issues that come with the development and implementation of artificial intelligence.

3.3.1   Data Privacy.

Data privacy has become a major concern as more aspects of our lives become digital and connected.

AI systems are often trained and enhanced with vast amounts of personal data, and this raises questions about consent, ownership, and protection.

The possibility of data breaches and misuse of personal information is a risk that needs to be managed proactively.

The application of regulations such as the General Data Protection Regulation (GDPR) in the European Union and other comparable laws around the world show an effort to balance the benefits provided by AI systems with the right to privacy.

There are also discussions about incorporating techniques such as differential privacy into AI algorithms to ensure that individual data is not exposed.

3.3.2   Work Automation

Automation, powered by AI, presents major transformations in the labor market. Some jobs may become obsolete, while new job categories emerge.

In this scenario, workers need to prepare for an economy that demands new skills, and education systems must adapt to provide the necessary training.

Additionally, there is concern about increasing economic inequality, as AI can disproportionately benefit those who have the skills and resources to take advantage of new technologies.

Public policies, such as the guarantee of a universal basic income or the tax on robots, have been suggested as ways to redistribute wealth and avoid widening income disparity.

3.3.3   Responsible and Ethical AI Development

The need for informed public debate and careful regulation is clear. Governments, businesses, and civil society must collaborate to create ethical guidelines and legal frameworks that not only encourage innovation, but also protect individual rights and foster social equity.

AI ethics encompasses a range of principles, such as transparency, fairness, non-discrimination, and accountability. Organizations such as the AI Now Institute, the Partnership on AI, and the IEEE have attempted to formalize these issues into sets of ethical and responsible practice guidelines for AI professionals and organizations.

Transparency is essential not only in terms of data protection but also in understanding the decisions made by AI.

Systems need to be explainable so that users can understand their workings and potential biases. Accountability is equally important; when an AI system makes a wrong decision, there should be mechanisms to assign responsibility and correct the error.

In short, while AI has the potential to bring about significant innovations, it also carries the risk of negative consequences, both anticipated and unpredictable.

Broad involvement, including regulators, industry professionals, academics, and the general public, is needed to ensure that the power of AI is used fairly and beneficially for all of society. This requires an ongoing process of evaluating and adapting ethical and policy norms, while advancing our understanding and application of AI technology.

3.4   Future.

The idea of a technological singularity, put forward by Kurzweil (2012) and other futurist thinkers, elicits both enthusiasm and caution when it comes to the potential of AI.

The singularity refers to a hypothetical future in which technological progress, driven by superintelligent artificial intelligences, accelerates beyond the human capacity to comprehend or control.

If superintelligent machines come into existence, they could solve complex problems with unparalleled efficiency, create new technologies that today seem impossible, and perhaps even answer fundamental questions about life, the universe, and consciousness.

This could usher in an era of abundance, where scarcity is eradicated and human capabilities are vastly expanded.

Proponents of this theory argue that AI could quickly overtake human intelligence, leading to exponential advances in science, engineering, and other fields.

However, this same superintelligence could present serious existential risks if not adequately controlled, a concern reflected in the efforts of organizations such as the Future of Life Institute and the Centre for the Study of Existential Risk.

In addition to concerns about the singularity, there are numerous other aspects of the future of AI that are the subject of reflection and planning.

These include:

1. Social integration and collaboration. How AI will be integrated into society and how it will collaborate with people at work, in home life, and in public decision-making.
2. Sustainable development. How AI can be used to combat climate change, promote environmental sustainability, and support a green economy.

3. Inclusion and diversity. How to ensure that the benefits of AI are distributed equitably, avoiding exclusion or worsening of existing inequalities.

4. Legal and security implications. Developing policies and protocols to maintain global security in the face of the emergence of powerful new technologies and protection against malicious uses of AI, such as in cyberattacks or authoritarian surveillance systems.

5. Evolution of the labor market. Preparation for the transition in the nature of work, with the displacement of certain professions and the creation of new ones, requiring new skill sets and adaptations both in the education system and in employment and social security policies.

6. Bioethics and AI. As AI begins to interact more with biology, through brain-machine interfaces and biotechnology, ethical issues become increasingly intricate and complex.

7. Politicization of AI. How nations will regulate and compete in the field of AI including issues of sovereignty, economic development, and global balance of power.

At the heart of these considerations is the understanding that AI is not a destination in itself, but a path that society is actively charting.

The choices about how to develop, implement, and regulate AI are critical and will have far-reaching implications for future generations.

The future of AI, therefore, is not only in the hands of those who develop the technology, but largely in the public policies that shape its use, in the ethical discussions that define its limits, and in the individual and collective choices that determine its impact on society.

By addressing these questions with insight and responsibility, we can strive to ensure a future where AI serves as a force for good, promoting human well-being and prosperity in a sustainable and equitable manner.

3.5   Notable concepts to underline.

1. Machine Learning. A subfield of artificial intelligence that allows computer systems to learn and evolve based on data without being explicitly programmed to perform specific tasks.

2. Neural Networks. Algorithms modeled from human neural connections that are used to recognize patterns and perform classification and regression tasks, which are fundamental in many machine learning applications.

3. Natural Language Processing (NLP). Branch of AI that focuses on the interaction between computers and human language, including language translation, speech recognition, and text generation.

4. Computer Vision. An area of artificial intelligence that is dedicated to making machines interpret and understand the visual content of the world, such as images and videos, with the aim of replicating the complexity of human vision.

5. Genetic Algorithm. A search and optimization technique based on principles of biological evolution, such as selection, crossbreeding, and mutation, to solve problems and optimize solutions.

6. Recommendation System. A type of information system that predicts a user's preference and suggests automated decision items or routes. Widely used in online retail, streaming services and other applications.

7. Autonomous Agents. Programs that can perform tasks or functions on behalf of a user with a certain independence, making their own decisions based on data and artificial intelligence.

8. Deep Learning. A set of machine learning algorithms that uses multiple layers of processing, including deep neural networks, to extract progressively more abstract features from data.

9. AI Ethics. This field of study is concerned with the morality of decisions made by AI systems, their societal implications, and issues such as algorithmic bias, fairness, and privacy.

10. Swarm Intelligence. A collective behavior emerging from decentralized, self-organizing systems, both natural and artificial, inspired by colonies of insects and other groups of animals to solve problems or optimize functionalities.

11. Cognitive Robotics. Area of study related to the inclusion of cognitive processes in robots, allowing them to learn from their experiences, recognize objects and understand commands or natural language.

12. Reinforcement Learning. Machine learning area where algorithms learn to make sequential decisions, experiencing actions in an environment, and receiving rewards or penalties based on the results.

13. Chatbot. A computer program that uses AI, especially natural language processing, to simulate a conversation with human users, either by text or voice.

14. Algorithmic Bias. Unintended biases in AI systems that can lead to discriminatory or unfair outcomes, typically reflecting bias in training data or algorithm formulation.

15. Artificial General Intelligence (AGI). The hypothetical skill level of a machine that could understand, learn, and apply intelligence to a diverse range of problems and tasks at a level comparable to or superior to that of a human.

16. IoT and AI (Internet of Things and Artificial Intelligence). The combination of the Internet of Things, which connects physical devices to the internet, with AI, which provides the ability to process data and make intelligent decisions autonomously.

17. Model Interpretability. The ability to understand and explain how AI models make decisions, which is especially important in fields such as medicine or law where decisions need to be understandable and justifiable.

18. Training Data. Dataset used to teach machine learning algorithms to recognize patterns and make decisions. The quality and diversity of this data is crucial to the performance of AI models.

19. Expert System. An AI application capable of emulating the decision of a human expert in a specific field, based on a set of rules and logics programmed to make complex decisions.

20. Computational Cognition. Study of how the human brain processes information and how these processes can be simulated in machines. It includes understanding perception, memory, attention, language, and problem-solving.

21. Text Mining. Process of extracting useful and meaningful information from large and complex texts using NLP methods and data analysis. Useful for sentiment analysis and recognition of named entities.

22. Computational Semantics. A branch of NLP that deals with the understanding and generation of meaning in natural language by machines, aiming to understand contextual issues and language nuances.

23. Intelligent Control. Application of AI in control systems to improve the performance of machines and processes that operate in complex and dynamic environments.

24. Multi-agent Simulation. Modeling environments with multiple autonomous agents interacting with each other, common in social AI research, games, and complex economic or ecological systems.

25. Autonomous Vehicles. AI-equipped vehicles capable of performing driving tasks without human intervention, combining sensing, NLP, computer vision, and intelligent control technologies.

These terms are the key to understanding the broad scope and depth of field of artificial intelligence and its various applications and challenges.

4 Integration of AI with other emerging technologies.

"Knowledge is power. Information is liberation."
Kofi Annan [1]

Artificial intelligence (AI), in its exponential growth trajectory, does not develop in a technological vacuum. On the contrary, the true power of AI is revealed when it is at the intersection of other emerging technologies, such as the Internet of Things (IoT), blockchain, and quantum computing.

These technological interactions not only amplify the capabilities of AI, but also open up a vast field of new applications, challenges, and ethical questions that shape the future of contemporary societies.

Understanding these synergies is crucial for any professional or scholar of artificial intelligence who wants to grasp the complexities of the digital age.

4.1 Artificial intelligence and the Internet of Things: the connection of the physical world to the digital world.

The Internet of Things (IoT) represents the extension of the digital network into the physical world, connecting everyday devices to the internet, allowing them to collect, send, and receive data.

---

[1] Kofi Annan was a Ghanaian diplomat who served as Secretary-General of the United Nations from 1997 to 2006. He was the seventh UN Secretary-General and the first African to hold that position. Annan was known for his commitment to peace, human rights, sustainable development, and prominent role in promoting the reform and effectiveness of the United Nations.

When associated with AI, IoT transcends mere data collection and acquires the ability to analyze, predict, and decide autonomously.

The integration of AI with IoT transforms the way we interact with the world around us. Smart cities, for example, are a direct manifestation of this integration, where sensors spread across an urban infrastructure collect real-time data on traffic, energy consumption, air quality, among other aspects.

AI processes this data, identifying patterns and generating insights that allow authorities to optimize resources, reduce emissions, and improve the quality of life of citizens (HOLLAND, 2019).

In the healthcare sector, the combination of AI and IoT has enhanced preventive and personalized medicine practices. Wearable devices, such as smartwatches, continuously monitor patients' vital signs, sending this data to AI systems that can identify anomalies and predict health crises before they even occur, allowing for faster and more accurate interventions (KULKARNI et al., 2017).

In manufacturing, the fusion of AI and IoT has resulted in the creation of smart factories, where machines equipped with sensors monitor production in real time. AI analyzes this data to predict failures, optimize processes, and reduce waste, leading to a significant increase in operational efficiency (LEE et al., 2018).

4.2   Artificial intelligence and blockchain: the revolution of trust and decentralization.

Blockchain, the technology underlying Bitcoin and other cryptocurrencies, is a decentralized network that allows for the creation of immutable and secure records.

AI, when integrated with blockchain, can use this infrastructure to ensure the transparency, security, and integrity of the data with which it operates.

One of the biggest concerns in the application of AI is data integrity and privacy. Blockchain offers a solution to these challenges by allowing data to be stored in a decentralized manner and protected from tampering.

This integration is particularly useful in areas such as digital identity management and product traceability in the supply chain, where trust and data veracity are essential (CASADO-VARA et al., 2018).

In the financial sector, the combination of AI and blockchain is transforming smart contract management, where AI algorithms can automatically monitor and execute contracts based on predefined conditions, with security guaranteed by blockchain.

This reduces the need for intermediaries, lowering costs and increasing efficiency (MCCALLIG et al., 2019).

In healthcare, AI can be applied to analyze large volumes of medical data stored on blockchains, ensuring that analyses are based on authentic and unadulterated information.

In addition, this combination can ensure that patient data is accessible only by authorized parties, respecting privacy and security standards (ENGELHARDT, 2017).

4.3   Artificial intelligence and quantum computing: the limit of computational capacity.

Quantum computing, still in its early stages, promises a revolution in the ability to process information. While classical computers operate with bits, which can represent 0 or 1, quantum computers use qubits, which can represent 0, 1, or both simultaneously, thanks to the phenomenon of quantum entanglement.

The combination of AI with quantum computing can result in significant advances in solving problems that require great computational power, such as optimizing complex neural networks, simulating molecules for drug discovery, and modeling financial systems (ARUTE et al., 2019).

However, this integration also presents unique challenges. The instability of qubits and the complexity of quantum algorithms are barriers that still need to be overcome.

However, as quantum technology advances, it is hoped that AI will be able to harness its power to perform previously unimaginable calculations, opening up new frontiers for science and technology (BOIXO et al., 2018).

4.4   The impact of technological convergence.

The convergence of AI with other emerging technologies is not without ethical implications. The expansion of AI capabilities through IoT, blockchain, and quantum computing increases accountability for the use of these technologies, especially when it comes to privacy, security, and social impact.

With AI controlling critical systems that directly impact human life, issues such as liability for system failures and algorithmic bias become even more complex.

The decentralization promoted by blockchain, for example, although it offers advantages, can also hinder the regulation and supervision of these technologies (ZYSKIND et al., 2015).

Looking to the future of AI integrated with these emerging technologies is to contemplate a horizon of almost limitless possibilities.

However, it is essential that the development of these technologies is guided by clear ethical principles, ensuring that technological innovations benefit humanity as a whole, without exacerbating inequalities or compromising fundamental rights.

5   Recommendation and personalization systems.

Recommendation systems have become an integral part of the contemporary digital experience, guiding users through vast seas of content and options.

From video and music streaming platforms such as Netflix and Spotify to e-commerce sites such as Amazon, these systems influence consumption decisions and shape user interaction with the digital world.

They personalize the content that each user sees, based on a detailed analysis of their previous behaviors and preferences.

The main purpose of a recommendation system is to predict a user's preferences for a set of items and suggest those that they are most likely to consume or enjoy.

These systems, which act as filters between the immensity of available options and the personalized user experience, operate based on complex machine learning algorithms and data mining techniques.

5.1   Collaborative filters: the power of the collective.

One of the most popular and effective methods in recommender systems is collaborative filtering, which can be divided into two main approaches: user-based and item-based.

1. User-based collaborative filter.

In this method, the system recommends items to a user based on items that other similar users (in terms of interaction history) have liked.

For example, if user A has watched and liked specific movies, and user B, who has a similar taste profile to user A, has liked other movies, those movies can be recommended to user A. This method is based on the hypothesis that users with similar tastes tend to like the same things.

2. Item-based collaborative filtering.

Unlike the user-based collaborative filter, this approach recommends items similar to those that the user has already liked.

For example, if a user has watched and liked a certain movie, the system will identify movies with similar characteristics (genre, actors, director) and recommend them to the user.

This method is widely used on e-commerce platforms, where similar items are suggested based on the user's purchase history.

3. Challenges of the collaborative filter.

Despite their effectiveness, collaborative filters face significant challenges, such as the "cold start" problem, which occurs when there is not enough data about a new user or item, making it difficult to generate accurate recommendations.

In addition, there is the scalability problem, since comparing all users or items can become computationally expensive on systems with millions of users and items.

5.2 Content-based systems: the world of structured data.

In addition to collaborative filters, another popular approach is the content-based system, which recommends items based on the characteristics of the items themselves and the preferences previously expressed by the user.

If a user usually watches science fiction movies, the system will analyze the characteristics of the movies (such as genre, theme, director) and recommend other movies that share these characteristics.

Content-based systems utilize natural language processing (NLP) and data analysis techniques to identify the characteristics of items and match them to the user's preferences.

However, these systems also face challenges, such as limiting the diversity of recommendations, since they tend to suggest items that are very similar to those the user has already consumed, which can result in a repetitive and monotonous user experience.

5.3 Hybrid systems: the best of both worlds.

To overcome the limitations of siloed methods, many recommendation systems take a hybrid approach, combining collaborative filters and content-based systems.

This combination allows the system to compensate for the weaknesses of each individual approach by offering more robust and diverse recommendations.

A classic example of a hybrid system is Netflix, which combines collaborative filters with content-based analysis to suggest movies and series that the user is most likely to like, considering both their personal preferences and the tendencies of users with similar profiles.

The personalization offered by recommendation systems brings undeniable benefits, such as a more relevant user experience and the discovery of new content that might otherwise go unnoticed. However, this personalization also raises ethical issues and significant challenges.

One of the main concerns is the creation of "filter bubbles," where users are only exposed to content that reinforces their existing preferences and viewpoints, limiting their exposure to new and diverse ideas.

This can have profound impacts, especially in areas such as politics and education, where diversity of information is crucial for the development of a critical and comprehensive view of the world (PARISER, 2011).

The massive collection of personal data required for personalization raises serious privacy concerns. Recommendation systems, when accessing and analyzing large volumes of user data, can inadvertently expose sensitive information or be used to manipulate consumer decisions, raising concerns about the design ethics of these systems (ZUBOFF, 2019).

Social media platforms and digital advertising often use recommendation systems to target specific ads to users, based on their online behavior.

While this practice can increase the relevance of ads, it can also exacerbate privacy issues and manipulation, as companies collect and use personal data in ways that users may not fully understand or consent to.

Recommendation systems are constantly evolving, and the future promises innovations that can mitigate some of today's challenges.

Technologies such as explainable artificial intelligence (XAI) are being developed to make recommendation algorithms more transparent and understandable, helping users understand how and why a recommendation was made.

5.4   Explainable artificial intelligence (XAI).

One of the most promising areas of innovation is explainable AI, which seeks to make recommendation models more transparent and provide clear and intuitive explanations for users about how their preferences were inferred and how recommendations were generated.

This can not only increase user trust in recommendation systems but also offer greater control over preferences and customizations.

Another emerging innovation is federated learning, which allows recommendation models to be trained on decentralized data while preserving user privacy.

Instead of collecting personal data on a central server, federated learning allows the data to remain on users' devices, with only the results of the training being shared.

This can significantly reduce the privacy risks associated with recommender systems (KONEČNÝ et al., 2016).

6 Unraveling the black box: interpretation and explainability of AI models.

Artificial intelligence, especially in its more advanced aspects such as deep learning, is often compared to a "black box."

This term describes the inherent complexity of many AI models, where decisions or predictions are produced by internal processes that are largely incomprehensible to humans.

In critical industries like healthcare and finance, this lack of transparency can have serious consequences, from poor medical decisions to financial collapse.

Interpretability and explainability in AI, therefore, are essential aspects to ensure that algorithmic decisions can be understood, audited, and trusted.

Explainable models allow users to understand the factors that influenced a particular decision, increasing confidence and making it easier to identify and correct potential biases or errors.

6.1 Interpretation and explainability techniques.

To deal with the complexity of AI models and make them more transparent, several techniques have been developed.

Among the most notable are LIME (Local Interpretable Model-agnostic Explanations) and SHAP (SHapley Additive exPlanations), which provide accessible explanations of how a model arrived at a specific decision.

1. LIME (Local Interpretable Model-agnostic Explanations).

LIME is a technique designed to explain the prediction of any AI model, regardless of its complexity.

It works by creating a simple, interpretable model (like a linear regression) that fits locally to the prediction you want to explain. In other words, it generates a simplified version of the model that can be understood by humans, but only in the vicinity of the specific prediction.

For example, in an image classification model that predicts whether or not an image contains a cat, LIME can identify which image features (such as edges or texture patterns) contributed most to this prediction.

This allows developers and users to understand which factors the model considers most important in decision-making (RIBEIRO et al., 2016).

2. SHAP (SHapley Additive exPlanations).

SHAP is based on Shapley's concept of values, a game theory solution that assigns each participant (in this case, each input trait) a fair contribution to the final outcome.

SHAP, therefore, provides a consistent and unified measure of the importance of each trait in relation to model prediction.

Unlike other techniques, SHAP offers a global explanation of the model, which means that it can provide insights not only into specific predictions, but also into how the model behaves in general.

This is particularly useful in sectors such as finance, where the explanation of complex algorithmic decisions, such as the granting of credit, must be clear and justified to avoid discrimination or unintentional bias (LUNDGREN et al., 2017).

Challenges and Limitations of Explainability Techniques

While explainability techniques like LIME and SHAP have advanced significantly, they also face challenges and limitations that must be considered.

6.2   Complexity and Interpretation.

One of the main criticisms of explainability techniques is that, although they make models more transparent, the explanation itself can become complex, especially for users without a technical background.

Explanations generated by LIME, for example, are only valid locally, which can be confusing for users if they try to generalize the explanation to other predictions.

1. Robustness of Explanations.

Another concern is the robustness of the explanations. In some cases, small changes in the input data can result in significant changes in the explanation provided by techniques such as LIME.

This raises questions about the stability of the explanations and the trust that users can place in them.

2. Trade-offs between Interpretability and Accuracy.

Finally, there is the trade-off between interpretability and accuracy. Simpler models, such as decision trees or linear regressions, are naturally more interpretable, but may not achieve the same level of accuracy as more complex models, such as deep neural networks.

Therefore, the choice of model and explainability technique should consider the balance between the need for a clear explanation and the need for robust performance.

6.3   The Future of Explainability in AI.

The field of explainability in AI continues to evolve, driven by the growing demand for transparency in automated systems. As AI models become more complex and ubiquitous in critical decisions, the need for effective explainability techniques becomes increasingly pressing.

1. Real-time explainability.

    One of the future trends is the development of techniques that can provide real-time explanations, allowing users to understand model decisions as they are made.

    This is particularly relevant in applications such as algorithmic trading in finance or medical diagnosis in emergency settings.

2. Explainability and algorithmic fairness.

    Another important direction is the focus on algorithmic fairness, where explainability techniques are used to identify and mitigate biases in AI models.

    This involves not only explaining the decisions but also ensuring that those decisions are fair and equitable for all users.

3. Integration with explainable AI (XAI).

Finally, the future of explainability in AI is closely linked to the development of explainable AI (XAI), an approach that aims to create models that are, by design, more transparent and interpretable, without compromising accuracy.

Integrating XAI with techniques such as LIME and SHAP can provide a solid foundation for building AI systems that are both powerful and understandable.

7 Conclusion.

As we come to the end of this journey through the fascinating universe of Artificial Intelligence, it is important to reflect on the impact and implications of this technology on our society, economy, and culture.

Artificial Intelligence is much more than simply algorithms and mathematical models; It represents a revolution that is redefining the way we interact with the world around us.

From the essential value of information as a fundamental raw material to the historical evolution of Artificial Intelligence and the ethical and regulatory challenges that permeate the field, each chapter of this book has led us down a path of learning and discovery.

We learned about the basic concepts, practical applications, large-scale language models, Machine Learning, the importance of data, and the relevance of ethics and transparency in the use of AI.

It is critical to recognize that AI is not just a technological tool, but rather a transformative force that will shape the future of our society.

As we move into the future of AI, it is crucial to consider not only the technological advancements but also the social, economic, and ethical impacts of these innovations.

The quality and trust in data, the security and privacy of information, the proper structuring of databases, and legal and regulatory compliance are aspects that must be carefully considered in the development and implementation of Artificial Intelligence projects.

The responsibility for ensuring that AI is used ethically, transparently, and responsibly lies with everyone involved in this innovation ecosystem.

As we say goodbye to this book and prepare to face the challenges and opportunities that AI has in store for us, I invite each of us to embrace the future with an open mind, creativity, and commitment to sustainable and inclusive development.

May we use the power of Artificial Intelligence to build a better, more connected and more harmonious world for future generations.

May Artificial Intelligence continue to challenge, surprise and transform us, and may this book serve as a compass for us to navigate with wisdom and discernment in this sea of innovation and discovery. May we reap the fruits of this shared knowledge and build together a fairer, more inclusive and sustainable world through the transformative power of Artificial Intelligence.

Thank you for taking the time and attention to explore this vast and exciting field of Artificial Intelligence with us. May the ideas and concepts presented in these pages continue to echo in your mind and heart, inspiring you to seek new horizons and break new ground on the journey towards the future of AI.

May curiosity, innovation, and collaboration guide your steps, and may Artificial Intelligence be a powerful ally in your quest for knowledge, growth, and transformation.

To all those who have dedicated themselves to this book and to those who have ventured into reading it, I wish them success, achievements and extraordinary discoveries.

The future is now. Let's shape it together, with wisdom, compassion, and vision.

This book is part of Prof. Marcão's Artificial Intelligence Collection, a series dedicated to exploring the complexities and implications of AI in contemporary society.

Available on Amazon, the collection offers an in-depth and critical look at the role of data, information, and knowledge in the age of artificial intelligence, serving as an indispensable resource for professionals, academics, and enthusiasts in the field.

8 FAQ.

1. Is artificial intelligence capable of learning and evolving on its own?

   Yes, artificial intelligence can learn and evolve on its own through algorithms and machine learning processes.

2. Is artificial intelligence a recent technology?

   Artificial intelligence is not a recent technology, but it has been developed and improved over the decades.

3. Can artificial intelligence be used in the area of security?

   Yes, artificial intelligence has been successfully applied in the area of security for threat detection and crime prevention.

4. Can artificial intelligence make moral decisions?

   Artificial intelligence cannot yet make moral decisions autonomously, as it lacks ethical and emotional understanding.

5. Can artificial intelligence completely replace human work?

   While artificial intelligence can automate repetitive tasks, it complements human labor, but does not necessarily replace it in its entirety.

6. Is artificial intelligence able to recognize patterns in large volumes of data?

   Yes, artificial intelligence is able to identify patterns and trends in large data sets more efficiently than humans.

7. Can artificial intelligence influence the way consumers interact with companies?

Yes, artificial intelligence has revolutionized the customer experience by enabling more personalized and efficient interactions with companies.

8. Does artificial intelligence have the potential to revolutionize the entertainment industry?

Yes, artificial intelligence is already being utilized in the entertainment industry for personalized recommendations, content creation, and more.

9. Does artificial intelligence pose risks to the privacy of individuals' data?

Yes, artificial intelligence can pose risks to data privacy if adequate security and information protection measures are not adopted.

10. Can artificial intelligence contribute to environmental sustainability?

Yes, artificial intelligence can assist in natural resource management, disaster prevention, and process optimization to promote environmental sustainability.

11. How is artificial intelligence applied in voice recognition?

Artificial intelligence is used in speech recognition through natural language processing algorithms that interpret and transcribe human speech.

12. How can artificial intelligence help prevent financial fraud?

Artificial intelligence can identify suspicious patterns in financial transactions, alerting to possible fraud and contributing to the security of the system.

13. How can artificial intelligence be used in education?

Artificial intelligence can personalize teaching, adapting content according to the pace and needs of each student, in addition to assisting in performance evaluation.

14. How can artificial intelligence be used to improve the user experience on online platforms?

Artificial intelligence can analyze user behavior, recommend relevant content, provide personalized support, and optimize navigation on online platforms.

15. How can artificial intelligence be used to optimize industrial processes?

Artificial intelligence can analyze large volumes of data in real time, identify failures, predict maintenance, and optimize production in industries.

16. How is artificial intelligence applied in autonomous vehicle driving?

Artificial intelligence is used in computer vision systems, sensors, and control algorithms to enable the autonomous driving of vehicles safely and efficiently.

17. How are chatbots used in customer interaction?

Chatbots are used to provide customer support, answer frequently asked questions, route requests, and conduct transactions in an automated and effective manner.

18. How can we ensure transparency and ethics in the use of artificial intelligence?

Ensuring transparency and ethics in the use of artificial intelligence requires the implementation of appropriate policies, regulations, and oversight, as well as the design of systems that are aligned with human values.

19. Is it possible for artificial intelligence to develop feelings?

Currently, artificial intelligence is unable to develop feelings, as it has no consciousness or emotions.

20. In what areas can artificial intelligence be applied in the agricultural sector?

Artificial intelligence can be applied in the agricultural sector to optimize irrigation, monitor crops, predict crop diseases, and increase productivity.

21. In what contexts can artificial intelligence be an ally in the legal field?

Artificial intelligence can be used in the legal field for legal research, case analysis, contract review, and automation of bureaucratic processes.

22. What is deep learning in artificial intelligence?

Deep learning is an artificial intelligence technique that utilizes deep neural networks to learn complex representations of data and perform sophisticated tasks.

23. What is weak AI and how is it different from strong AI?

Weak artificial intelligence refers to AI systems that specialize in specific tasks, while strong AI seeks to replicate human intelligence across the board.

24. What is natural language processing and how does artificial intelligence use it?

Natural language processing is the ability of the machine to understand and process human language. Artificial intelligence uses it for machine translation, sentiment analysis in texts, among others.

25. What are robots with artificial intelligence and how are they employed?

Robots with artificial intelligence are machines capable of making decisions based on data and learning from interaction with the environment.

They are employed in tasks such as industrial assembly, home care, and even surgery.

26. What are expert systems and how do they contribute to artificial intelligence?

Expert systems are computer programs that use rules and logic to solve complex problems in specific areas. They contribute to artificial intelligence by providing accurate and specialized solutions.

27. What are unmanned vehicles and how is artificial intelligence involved?

Unmanned vehicles are vehicles that can move around without the presence of a human driver. Artificial intelligence is essential for the operation of these vehicles, as it allows the interpretation of sensor data, navigation decision-making, and obstacle avoidance.

28. What are the ethical implications of the use of artificial intelligence in the area of security?

The ethical implications of using artificial intelligence in the area of security include issues related to privacy, algorithmic discrimination, human oversight, transparency of systems, and accountability for decision-making.

29. What are the main applications of artificial intelligence in healthcare?

The main applications of artificial intelligence in healthcare include medical diagnosis, medical image analysis, drug discovery, patient record management, and treatment personalization.

30. What are the challenges of artificial intelligence in dealing with the interpretation and understanding of human language?

The challenges of artificial intelligence in dealing with the interpretation and understanding of human language involve ambiguity, context, irony, sarcasm, sentiment, and the different nuances of verbal and written communication.

31. What are the impacts of artificial intelligence on the global economy and the labor market?

The impacts of artificial intelligence on the global economy and the labor market include the automation of tasks, the creation of new jobs, the need for professional retraining, and the redefinition of skills required by the market.

32. What are the main machine learning algorithms used in artificial intelligence?

The main machine learning algorithms used in artificial intelligence include linear regression, decision trees, neural networks, support vector machines, genetic algorithms, and clustering algorithms.

33. What are the risks of bias and discrimination associated with artificial intelligence?

The risks of bias and discrimination associated with artificial intelligence include the reproduction of biases present in the data used for training, unfair discrimination in automated decisions, lack of diversity in the creation of systems, and difficulty in explaining how decisions were made.

34. What skills are needed to work with artificial intelligence?

To work with artificial intelligence, skills in programming, mathematics, statistics, data science, analytical thinking, problem-solving, curiosity, communication skills, and continuous learning capacity are required.

35. What are the differences between artificial intelligence and automation?

Artificial intelligence refers to the ability of computer systems to perform tasks that would normally require human intelligence, while automation refers to performing tasks automatically, without necessarily involving intelligence.

36. What are the applications of AI in the personalization of services and products?

The applications of AI in the personalization of services and products include recommending products on e-commerce platforms, suggesting content on social networks, customizing user experiences in applications, and adapting services according to individual preferences.

37. What are the differences between supervised and unsupervised learning in machine learning?

In supervised learning, algorithms are trained with labeled data, i.e., the correct answers are provided, while in unsupervised learning, algorithms are trained with unlabeled data, allowing for the identification of patterns and structures in the data.

38. What are the future trends in artificial intelligence?

Future trends in artificial intelligence include advances in robotics, the integration of AI into everyday devices, developments in natural language processing systems, the use of AI for more accurate predictions, and the development of ethical and responsible models.

39. How is artificial intelligence being used to combat climate change?

Artificial intelligence is being used to analyze large environmental datasets, predict weather patterns, monitor deforestation, optimize energy use, and propose solutions to reduce greenhouse gas emissions.

40. How is artificial intelligence employed in the area of cybersecurity?

Artificial intelligence is employed in the field of cybersecurity to identify patterns of malicious activity, detect attacks in real time, mitigate vulnerabilities, strengthen data protection, and respond quickly to potential threats.

41. What is the role of artificial intelligence in the creation of smart cities?

Artificial intelligence plays a key role in creating smart cities by enabling real-time data collection and analysis, optimizing traffic, managing waste, improving energy efficiency, and promoting the quality of life for citizens.

42. How can artificial intelligence contribute to improving energy efficiency?

Artificial intelligence can contribute to improving energy efficiency by optimizing energy consumption in buildings, predicting demands, identifying potential waste, managing smart grids, and encouraging sustainable practices.

43. What is the importance of ethics in the research and development of artificial intelligence?

Ethics plays a crucial role in artificial intelligence research and development, as it guides the creation of fair, transparent, accountable systems that respect human rights and ensure the security and privacy of users.

44. How can artificial intelligence be applied in the diagnosis of diseases?

Artificial intelligence can be applied in the diagnosis of diseases through the analysis of symptoms, medical images, laboratory tests, and patient history, assisting healthcare professionals in the early and accurate identification of medical conditions.

45. What is the impact of artificial intelligence on the customer service sector?

Artificial intelligence has a significant impact on the customer service industry by enabling the automation of interactions, offering real-time support, personalizing service, reducing wait times, and improving customer satisfaction.

46. How can artificial intelligence help detect financial fraud?

Artificial intelligence can assist in the detection of financial fraud by analyzing patterns of behavior, identifying suspicious transactions, monitoring irregular activity, and preventing fraudulent activity in real-time.

47. What are the main ethical challenges of using artificial intelligence in the area of justice?

The main ethical challenges of using artificial intelligence in the area of justice include ensuring the impartiality and transparency of algorithms, preventing algorithmic discrimination, ensuring the protection of individual rights and ensuring accountability for automated decisions.

48. How can Artificial Intelligence assist in the development of new materials?

Artificial Intelligence can assist in the development of new materials through computer modeling, prediction of physical and chemical properties, search for optimized combinations of elements, and accelerate the process of discovering and designing new materials.

49. How can artificial intelligence contribute to the personalization of medical treatments?

Artificial intelligence can contribute to the personalization of medical treatments by analyzing genetic data, patient medical history, and response to therapies, allowing for the creation of more effective treatment approaches tailored to individual needs.

50. What is the importance of the interpretability of artificial intelligence models?

The interpretability of artificial intelligence models is essential to understand how algorithms work, explain the decisions made, identify potential biases, ensure user trust, and facilitate adoption and acceptance of the technology.

51. How can artificial intelligence be used to predict market trends?

Artificial intelligence can be used to predict market trends by analyzing consumer data, consumer behavior, sales history, competitor information, and other relevant factors, providing insights for strategic decision-making.

52. What are the implications of using artificial intelligence algorithms in education?

The implications of using artificial intelligence algorithms in education include personalizing teaching, adapting content, evaluating performance, identifying learning difficulties, managing classrooms, and creating more effective and inclusive learning environments.

53. How can artificial intelligence be applied in the automation of administrative processes?

Artificial intelligence can be applied in the automation of administrative processes through document interpretation, report generation, automation of repetitive tasks, workflow management, and optimization of operational efficiency in companies and organizations.

9 References.

ABBOTT, R. (2016). I Think, Therefore I Invent. Creative Computers and the Future of Patent Law. Boston College Law Review.

ALPAYDIN, E. (2020). Introduction to Machine Learning (4th ed.). MIT Press.

ARUTE, F., et al. (2019). Quantum Supremacy Using a Programmable Superconducting Processor. Nature, 574(7779), 505-510.

BENDER, E.M., GEBRU, T., MCMILLAN-MAJOR, A., & MITCHELL, M. (2021). On the Dangers of Stochastic Parrots: Can Language Models Be Too Big? In Proceedings of the 2021 ACM Conference on Fairness, Accountability, and Transparency (pp. 610-623). ACM.

BERKOVSKY, K. Yu, S. CONWAY, D. TAIB, R., ZHOU, J. and CHEN, F. (2018). Do I trust a machine? Differences in user trust based on system performance, in. Human and Machine Learning, Springer, 245–264.

BOIXO, S., ISHIMOTO, S., et al. (2018). Characterizing Quantum Supremacy in Near-Term Devices. Nature Physics, 14, 595-600.

CHEN, M., WEI, Z., HUANG, Z., DING, B., & LI, Y. (2020) Simple and deep graph convolutional networks. In ICML.

DOSHI-VELEZ, F., & KIM, B. (2017). Towards A Rigorous Science of Interpretable Machine Learning. arXiv preprint arXiv.1702.08608. Available at https.//arxiv.org/abs/1702.08608.

GOERTZEL, B. (2014). Artificial general intelligence. concept, state of the art, and future prospects. Journal of Artificial General Intelligence, 5(1), 1.

GUO, B., Zhang, X., WANG, Z., Jiang, M., NIE, J., DING, Y., YUE, J., & Wu, Y. (2023). How close is ChatGPT to human experts? Comparison corpus, evaluation, and detection. ar Xiv preprint arXiv.2301.07597.

I., & MITCHELL, T. M. (2015). Machine learning. Trends, perspectives, and prospects. Science, 349(6245), 255-260.

KROLL, J.A., et al. (2017). Accountable algorithms. University of Pennsylvania Law Review, 165(3), 633-705.

KULKARNI, A. P., VENKATESH, M., & ZHOU, B. (2017). AI in Healthcare: The IoT-Wearable Devices Connection. Proceedings of the IEEE International Conference on Artificial Intelligence Circuits and Systems, 1-3.

KURZWEIL, R. (2012). How to Create a Mind. The Secret of Human Thought Revealed. Gerald Duckworth & Co Ltd.

LAW, E. and AHN, L.v. (2011) Human computation, Vol. 5, Morgan & Claypool Publishers, pp. 1–121.

LE CUN, Y., BOSER, B., DENKER, J.S., HENDERSON, D., HOWARD, R.E., HUBBARD, W., & JACKEL, L.D. (1989). Backpropagation Applied to Handwritten Zip Code Recognition. Neural Computation, 1(4), 541-551.

LEE, A. (2019). The Role of Data Structuring in Machine Learning. Journal of Artificial Intelligence, 20(3), 45-58.

MITCHELL, Margaret. Ethical AI in Education: Challenges and Opportunities. San Francisco: Google Press, 2020.

MITTELSTADT, B. D., ALLO, P., & FLORIDI, L. (2016). The ethics of algorithms. Mapping the debate. In Data & Society Initiative. Oxford. Oxford Internet Institute.

MURPHY, K. P. (2012). Machine learning. a probabilistic perspective. MIT press.

MURPHY, R. R. (2019). Introduction to AI Robotics (2nd ed.). MIT Press.

NOBLE, S.U. (2018). Algorithms of Oppression. How Search Engines Reinforce Racism. New York University Press.

O'NEIL, Cathy & SCHUTT, Rachel. (2013). Doing Data Science. Sevastopol, CA. O'Reilly Media.

PARISER, E. (2011). The Filter Bubble: What the Internet Is Hiding from You. Penguin Press.

RADFORD, A., NARASIMHAN, K., SALIMANS, T., & SUTSKEVER, I. (2018). Improving Language Understanding by Generative Pretraining. OpenAI.

REDMAN, T.C. & SOARES, D. D. (2021). Application of AI in Data Governance. AI Magazine, 37(4), 78-85.

RUSSELL, S., & NORVIG, P. (2016). Artificial Intelligence. A Modern Approach (3rd ed.). Pearson Education.

SHALEV-SHWARTZ, S., & BEN-DAVID, S. (2014). Understanding Machine Learning. From Theory to Algorithms. Cambridge University Press.

SMITH, J. (2020). The Role of Databases in Artificial Intelligence. Journal of Data Science, 15(2), 123-136.

SUTTON, R. S., & BARTO, A. G. (2018). Reinforcement learning. An introduction. Bradford Books

TURING, A. (1950). Computing Machinery and Intelligence. In fashion. Mind, Volume 59, Number 236, pp. 433-460. Edinburgh. Thomas Nelson & Sons.

TURING, A.M. (1950). Computing Machinery and Intelligence. Mind, 59(236), 433-460.

YAMADA, I., ASAI, A., SHINDO, H., TAKEDA, H., & MATSUMOTO, Y. (2020). LUKE: Deep Contextualized Entity Representations with Entity-aware Self-attention. In Proceedings of the 2020 Conference on Empirical Methods in Natural Language Processing (EMNLP).

10 Discover the Complete Collection "Artificial Intelligence and the Power of Data" – An Invitation to Transform Your Career and Knowledge.

The "Artificial Intelligence and the Power of Data" Collection was created for those who want not only to understand Artificial Intelligence (AI), but also to apply it strategically and practically.

In a series of carefully crafted volumes, I unravel complex concepts in a clear and accessible manner, ensuring the reader has a thorough understanding of AI and its impact on modern societies.

No matter what your level of familiarity with the topic is, this collection turns the difficult into didactic, the theoretical into the applicable, and the technical into something powerful for your career.

10.1   Why buy this collection?

We are living through an unprecedented technological revolution, where AI is the driving force in areas such as medicine, finance, education, government, and entertainment.

The collection "Artificial Intelligence and the Power of Data" dives deep into all these sectors, with practical examples and reflections that go far beyond traditional concepts.

You'll find both the technical expertise and the ethical and social implications of AI encouraging you to see this technology not just as a tool, but as a true agent of transformation.

Each volume is a fundamental piece of this innovative puzzle: from machine learning to data governance and from ethics to practical application.

With the guidance of an experienced author who combines academic research with years of hands-on practice, this collection is more than a set of books – it's an indispensable guide for anyone looking to navigate and excel in this burgeoning field.

10.2   Target Audience of this Collection?

This collection is for everyone who wants to play a prominent role in the age of AI:

- ✓ Tech Professionals: Receive deep technical insights to expand their skills.

- ✓ Students and the Curious: have access to clear explanations that facilitate the understanding of the complex universe of AI.

- ✓ Managers, business leaders, and policymakers will also benefit from the strategic vision on AI, which is essential for making well-informed decisions.

- ✓ Professionals in Career Transition: Professionals in career transition or interested in specializing in AI will find here complete material to build their learning trajectory.

10.3   Much More Than Technique – A Complete Transformation.

This collection is not just a series of technical books; It is a tool for intellectual and professional growth.

With it, you go far beyond theory: each volume invites you to a deep reflection on the future of humanity in a world where machines and algorithms are increasingly present.

This is your invitation to master the knowledge that will define the future and become part of the transformation that Artificial Intelligence brings to the world.

Be a leader in your industry, master the skills the market demands, and prepare for the future with the "Artificial Intelligence and the Power of Data" collection.

This is not just a purchase; It is a decisive investment in your learning and professional development journey.

Prof. Marcão - Marcus Vinícius Pinto

M.Sc. in Information Technology.

Specialist in Artificial Intelligence, Data Governance and Information Architecture.

11 The Books of the Collection.

11.1 Data, Information and Knowledge in the era of Artificial Intelligence.

This book essentially explores the theoretical and practical foundations of Artificial Intelligence, from data collection to its transformation into intelligence. It focuses primarily on machine learning, AI training, and neural networks.

11.2 From Data to Gold: How to Turn Information into Wisdom in the Age of AI.

This book offers a critical analysis on the evolution of Artificial Intelligence, from raw data to the creation of artificial wisdom, integrating neural networks, deep learning, and knowledge modeling.

It presents practical examples in health, finance, and education, and addresses ethical and technical challenges.

11.3 Challenges and Limitations of Data in AI.

The book offers an in-depth analysis of the role of data in the development of AI exploring topics such as quality, bias, privacy, security, and scalability with practical case studies in healthcare, finance, and public safety.

11.4   Historical Data in Databases for AI: Structures, Preservation, and Purge.

This book investigates how historical data management is essential to the success of AI projects. It addresses the relevance of ISO standards to ensure quality and safety, in addition to analyzing trends and innovations in data processing.

11.5   Controlled Vocabulary for Data Dictionary: A Complete Guide.

This comprehensive guide explores the advantages and challenges of implementing controlled vocabularies in the context of AI and information science. With a detailed approach, it covers everything from the naming of data elements to the interactions between semantics and cognition.

11.6   Data Curation and Management for the Age of AI.

This book presents advanced strategies for transforming raw data into valuable insights, with a focus on meticulous curation and efficient data management. In addition to technical solutions, it addresses ethical and legal issues, empowering the reader to face the complex challenges of information.

11.7   Information Architecture.

The book addresses data management in the digital age, combining theory and practice to create efficient and scalable AI systems, with insights into modeling and ethical and legal challenges.

11.8   Fundamentals: The   Essentials   of   Mastering   Artificial Intelligence.

An essential work for anyone who wants to master the key concepts of AI, with an accessible approach and practical examples. The book explores innovations such as Machine Learning and Natural Language Processing, as well as ethical and legal challenges, and offers a clear view of the impact of AI on various industries.

11.9   LLMS - Large-Scale Language Models.

This essential guide helps you understand the revolution of Large-Scale Language Models (LLMs) in AI.

The book explores the evolution of GPTs and the latest innovations in human-computer interaction, offering practical insights into their impact on industries such as healthcare, education, and finance.

11.10   Machine Learning: Fundamentals and Advances.

This book offers a comprehensive overview of supervised and unsupervised algorithms, deep neural networks, and federated learning. In addition to addressing issues of ethics and explainability of models.

11.11   Inside Synthetic Minds.

This book reveals how these 'synthetic minds' are redefining creativity, work, and human interactions. This work presents a detailed analysis of the challenges and opportunities provided by these technologies, exploring their profound impact on society.

11.12   The Issue of Copyright.

This book invites the reader to explore the future of creativity in a world where human-machine collaboration is a reality, addressing questions about authorship, originality, and intellectual property in the age of generative AIs.

11.13   1121 Questions and Answers: From Basic to Complex – Part 1 to 4.

Organized into four volumes, these questions serve as essential practical guides to mastering key AI concepts.

Part 1 addresses information, data, geoprocessing, the evolution of artificial intelligence, its historical milestones and basic concepts.

Part 2 delves into complex concepts such as machine learning, natural language processing, computer vision, robotics, and decision algorithms.

Part 3 addresses issues such as data privacy, work automation, and the impact of large-scale language models (LLMs).

Part 4 explores the central role of data in the age of artificial intelligence, delving into the fundamentals of AI and its applications in areas such as mental health, government, and anti-corruption.

11.14   The Definitive Glossary of Artificial Intelligence.

This glossary presents more than a thousand artificial intelligence concepts clearly explained, covering topics such as Machine Learning, Natural Language Processing, Computer Vision, and AI Ethics.

- Part 1 contemplates concepts starting with the letters A to D.
- Part 2 contemplates concepts initiated by the letters E to M.
- Part 3 contemplates concepts starting with the letters N to Z.

11.15   Prompt Engineering - Volumes 1 to 6.

This collection covers all the fundamentals of prompt engineering, providing a complete foundation for professional development.

With a rich variety of prompts for areas such as leadership, digital marketing, and information technology, it offers practical examples to improve clarity, decision-making, and gain valuable insights.

The volumes cover the following subjects:

- Volume 1: Fundamentals. Structuring Concepts and History of Prompt Engineering.
- Volume 2: Tools and Technologies, State and Context Management, and Ethics and Security.
- Volume 3: Language Models, Tokenization, and Training Methods.
- Volume 4: How to Ask Right Questions.
- Volume 5: Case Studies and Errors.
- Volume 6: The Best Prompts.

11.16   Guide to Being a Prompt Engineer – Volumes 1 and 2.

The collection explores the advanced fundamentals and skills required to be a successful prompt engineer, highlighting the benefits, risks, and the critical role this role plays in the development of artificial intelligence.

Volume 1 covers crafting effective prompts, while Volume 2 is a guide to understanding and applying the fundamentals of Prompt Engineering.

11.17   Data Governance with AI – Volumes 1 to 3.

Find out how to implement effective data governance with this comprehensive collection. Offering practical guidance, this collection covers everything from data architecture and organization to protection and quality assurance, providing a complete view to transform data into strategic assets.

Volume 1 addresses practices and regulations. Volume 2 explores in depth the processes, techniques, and best practices for conducting effective audits on data models. Volume 3 is your definitive guide to deploying data governance with AI.

11.18   Algorithm Governance.

This book looks at the impact of algorithms on society, exploring their foundations and addressing ethical and regulatory issues. It addresses transparency, accountability, and bias, with practical solutions for auditing and monitoring algorithms in sectors such as finance, health, and education.

From IT Professional to AI Expert: The Ultimate Guide to a Successful

Career Transition.

For Information Technology professionals, the transition to AI represents a unique opportunity to enhance skills and contribute to the development of innovative solutions that shape the future.

In this book, we investigate the reasons for making this transition, the essential skills, the best learning path, and the prospects for the future of the IT job market.

11.19   Intelligent Leadership with AI: Transform Your Team and Drive Results.

This book reveals how artificial intelligence can revolutionize team management and maximize organizational performance.

By combining traditional leadership techniques with AI-powered insights, such as predictive analytics-based leadership, you'll learn how to optimize processes, make more strategic decisions, and create more efficient and engaged teams.

11.20   Impacts and Transformations: Complete Collection.

This collection offers a comprehensive and multifaceted analysis of the transformations brought about by Artificial Intelligence in contemporary society.

- Volume 1: Challenges and Solutions in the Detection of Texts Generated by Artificial Intelligence.
- Volume 2: The Age of Filter Bubbles. Artificial Intelligence and the Illusion of Freedom.
- Volume 3: Content Creation with AI - How to Do It?
- Volume 4: The Singularity Is Closer Than You Think.

- Volume 5: Human Stupidity versus Artificial Intelligence.
- Volume 6: The Age of Stupidity! A Cult of Stupidity?
- Volume 7: Autonomy in Motion: The Intelligent Vehicle Revolution.
- Volume 8: Poiesis and Creativity with AI.
- Volume 9: Perfect Duo: AI + Automation.
- Volume 10: Who Holds the Power of Data?

11.21 Big Data with AI: Complete Collection.

The collection covers everything from the technological fundamentals and architecture of Big Data to the administration and glossary of essential technical terms.

The collection also discusses the future of humanity's relationship with the enormous volume of data generated in the databases of training in Big Data structuring.

- Volume 1: Fundamentals.
- Volume 2: Architecture.
- Volume 3: Implementation.
- Volume 4: Administration.
- Volume 5: Essential Themes and Definitions.
- Volume 6: Data Warehouse, Big Data, and AI.

12 About the Author.

I'm Marcus Pinto, better known as Prof. Marcão, a specialist in information technology, information architecture and artificial intelligence.

With more than four decades of dedicated work and research, I have built a solid and recognized trajectory, always focused on making technical knowledge accessible and applicable to all those who seek to understand and stand out in this transformative field.

My experience spans strategic consulting, education and authorship, as well as an extensive performance as an information architecture analyst.

This experience enables me to offer innovative solutions adapted to the constantly evolving needs of the technological market, anticipating trends and creating bridges between technical knowledge and practical impact.

Over the years, I have developed comprehensive and in-depth expertise in data, artificial intelligence, and information governance – areas that have become essential for building robust and secure systems capable of handling the vast volume of data that shapes today's world.

My book collection, available on Amazon, reflects this expertise, addressing topics such as Data Governance, Big Data, and Artificial Intelligence with a clear focus on practical applications and strategic vision.

Author of more than 150 books, I investigate the impact of artificial intelligence in multiple spheres, exploring everything from its technical bases to the ethical issues that become increasingly urgent with the adoption of this technology on a large scale.

In my lectures and mentorships, I share not only the value of AI, but also the challenges and responsibilities that come with its implementation – elements that I consider essential for ethical and conscious adoption.

I believe that technological evolution is an inevitable path. My books are a proposed guide on this path, offering deep and accessible insights for those who want not only to understand, but to master the technologies of the future.

With a focus on education and human development, I invite you to join me on this transformative journey, exploring the possibilities and challenges that this digital age has in store for us.

13 How to Contact Prof. Marcão.

13.1   For lectures, training and business mentoring.

marcao.tecno@gmail.com

13.2   Prof. Marcão, on Linkedin.

https://bit.ly/linkedin_profmarcao